THE GRANDMOTHER EFFECT

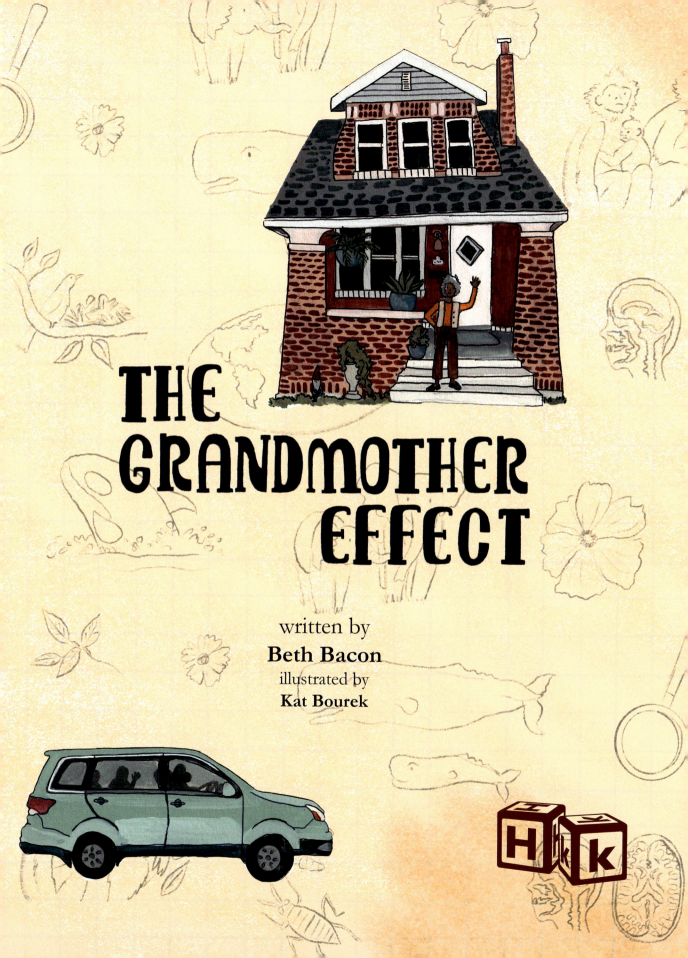

THE GRANDMOTHER EFFECT

written by
Beth Bacon

illustrated by
Kat Bourek

Histria Kids

Las Vegas - Chicago - Palm Beach

Published in the United States of America by
Histria Books
7181 N. Hualapai Way, Ste. 130-86
Las Vegas, NV 89166 USA
HistriaBooks.com

Histria Kids is an imprint of Histria Books. Titles published under the imprints of Histria Books are distributed worldwide.

All rights reserved. No part of this book may be reprinted or reproduced or utilized in any form or by any electronic, mechanical or other means, now known or hereafter invented, including photocopying and recording, or in any information storage or retrieval system, without the permission in writing from the Publisher.

Library of Congress Control Number: 2023948273

ISBN: 978-1-59211-383-5 (casebound)
ISBN: 978-1-59211-404-7 (eBook)

Text copyright © 2024 by Beth Bacon
Illustrations copyright © 2024 by Kat Bourek

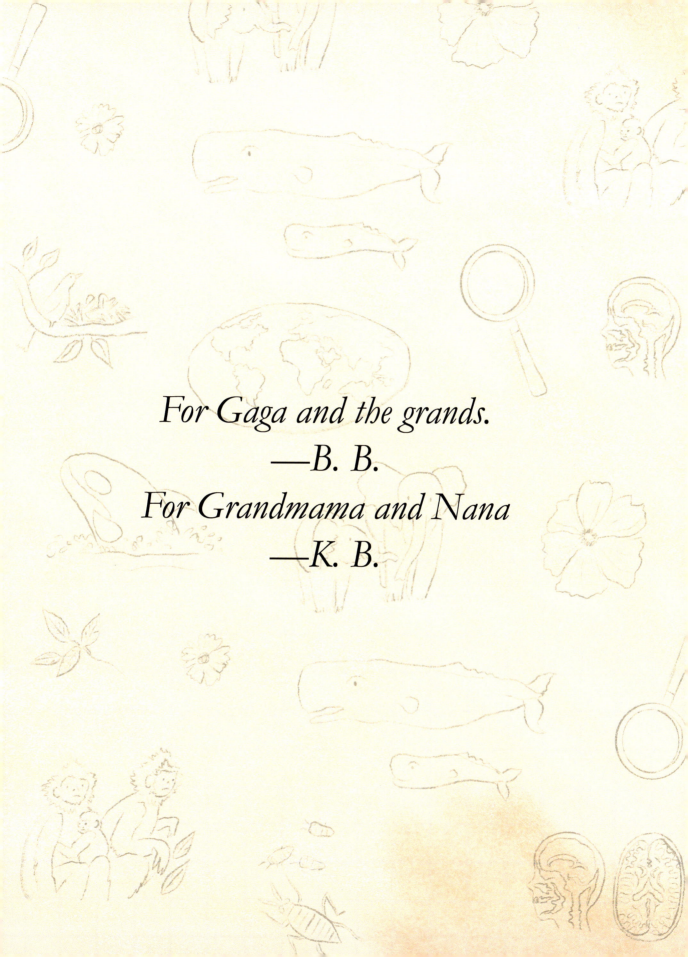

For Gaga and the grands.
—B. B.
For Grandmama and Nana
—K. B.

THE GRANDMOTHER EFFECT

Something wonderful happens

when we spend time with our grandmothers.

What happens, exactly?

It's not easy to measure.

It can't be
bought in a store.

But you can feel it

as surely as a soft breeze
on a spring afternoon.

It's like a secret ingredient in your favorite recipe.

You can always tell it's there.

Or loud enough
to raise the roof.

It can be splashy and daring.

Or cozy and warm.

An afternoon with your grandmother might be full of ups and downs.

But it's more than just fun and games.

You see, in the natural world, most animals

don't grow up with grandmothers.

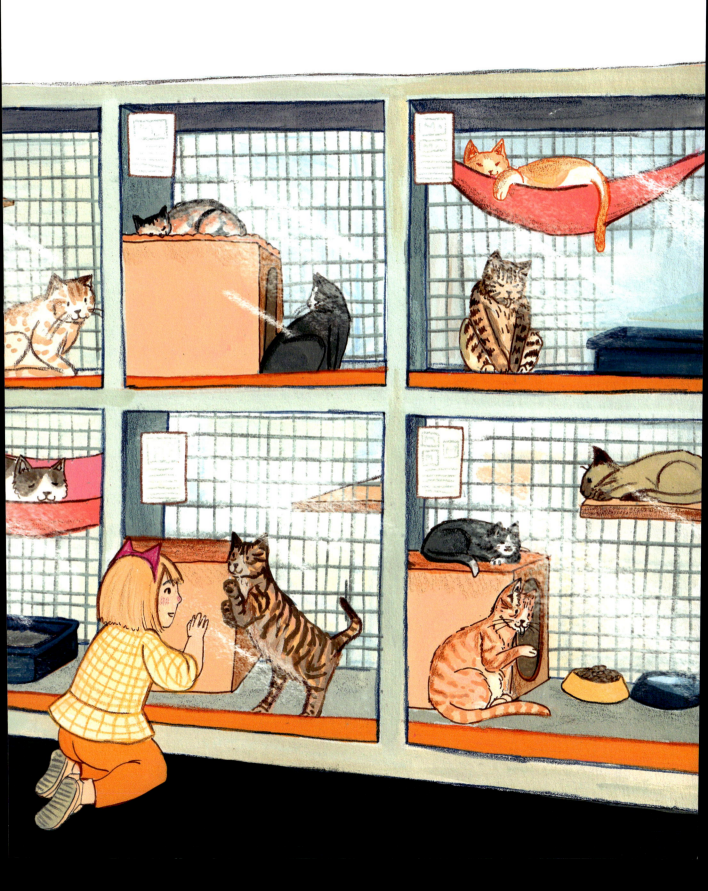

Tiny aphids have grandmothers.
Giant elephants and whales do, too.
But other than that, not many animals
have grandmothers.

So it's pretty special that we humans get to share our lives with grandmothers.

Some scientists who study fossils, animals, and archaeology have made an interesting discovery about grandmothers.

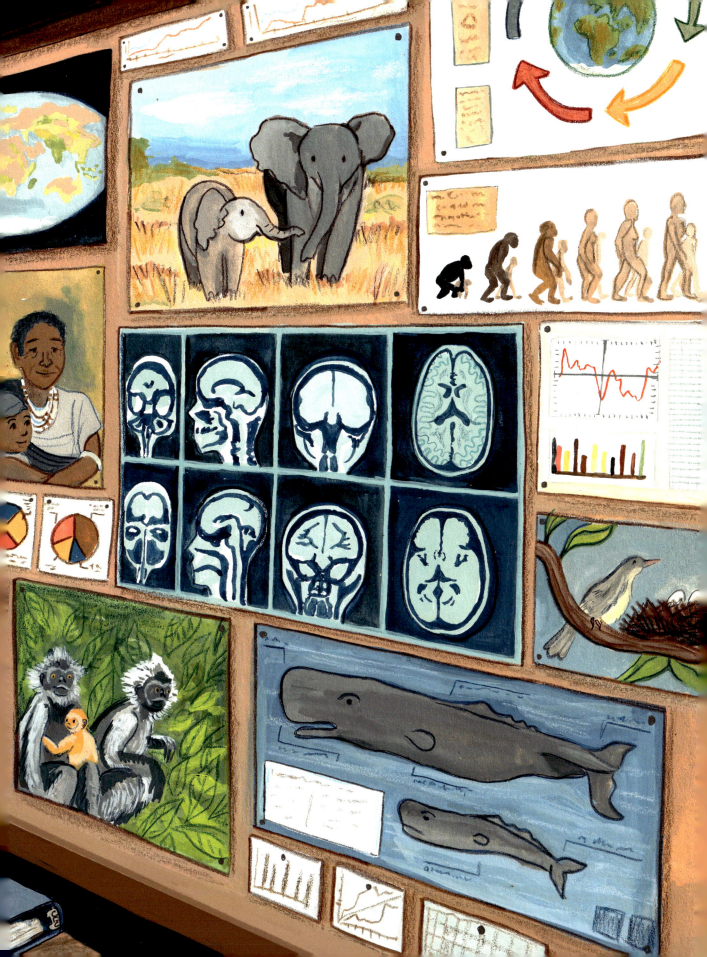

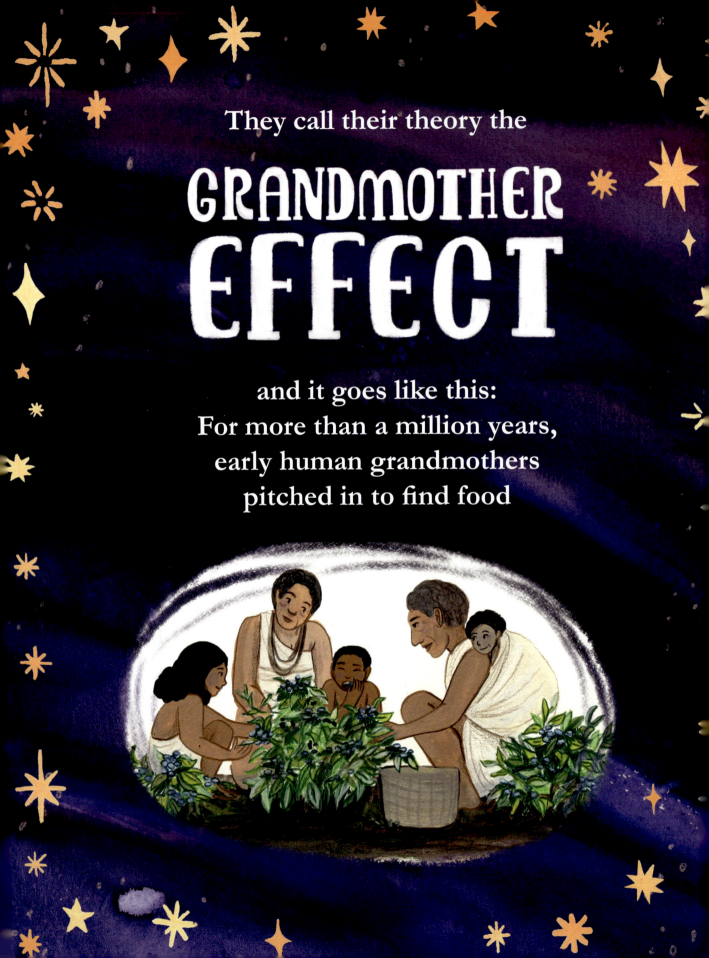

Over time, this allowed us to develop language, art, and science. When you think about it,

creative thinking and scientific discovery are things that only humans can do.

It turns out, grandmothers
are a big part of so many
things that make humans, human.

having fun,

or asking questions,

exploring, discovering, or performing

doesn't just feel good. It's actually super valuable. So the next time you see your grandmother,

give her an extra hug,
for having a special
place in human history—

simply by sharing her time and her love with you.

End Note
About The Scientific Theory Called "The Grandmother Effect"

Human evolution is the process in history that led to the development of our species: Homo sapiens. Scientists who are interested in human evolution study many different things including hunter-gatherer societies, fossil records from about 2 million years ago, and animals like chimpanzees, whales, elephants, and insects.

All that research has led some scientists to hypothesize that human grandmothers have long played a very valuable, very helpful role in the evolution of our species—and that has led to many important effects. They named this hypothesis "The Grandmother Effect."

Thanks to grandmothers, our species was able to develop large brains, form social groups, live long lives, and establish other important qualities—like language, creativity, and scientific exploration.

Today, grandmothers remain an important, and very special part of our lives.

Beth Bacon

Author Beth Bacon empowers today's kids to learn about themselves and the world through reading. Her books include *The Panda Cub Swap, The Book No One Wants To Read,* and *Alphabuddies: G Is First.* She is available for in-person and online author visits. Contact Beth at **www.BethBaconAuthor.com.**

Kat Bourek

Kat Bourek is an illustrator, arts educator, and avid urban-sketcher/knitter/cat lover/museum-enthusiast living in St. Louis, MO. She especially enjoys illustrating nonfiction materials that support inclusivity and the history of people, animals, and the environment. You can find more of her work at **www.katbourek.com** or follow her on social media @katbourek.